Table of Contents

Introduction

Antibiotics are used to kill or inhibit bacteria growth. Although you might think of antibiotics as modern medicine, they've actually been around for centuries. The original antibiotics, like a lot of today's antibiotics, are derived from natural sources. Certain plant extracts, essential oils, and even foods have antibiotic properties. For example, some food and vegetable extracts can prevent the growth of bacteria in food. Sometimes, these properties extend beyond the food and can aid in your personal hygiene. Cranberry extract contains both antibacterial and antioxidant compounds, making it a home remedy for urinary tract infections (UTIs). Herbs can be antibiotics, too. A small sampling study of 58 Chinese plants found that 23 had antibacterial properties and 15 had antifungal properties. A 2014 study found that an herbal therapy was just as effective as a chemical antibiotic in treating a small intestine bacterial overgrowth disorder.Since ancient times, herbs have been used as natural treatments for various illnesses, including viral infections. Due to their concentration of potent plant compounds, many herbs help fight viruses and are favored by practitioners of natural medicine. At the same time, the benefits of some herbs are only supported by limited human research, so you should take them with a grain of salt.Some herbs have powerful antiviral properties.

Antibiotics Foods

Honey

Honey is one the oldest known antibiotics, tracing back to ancient times. Egyptians frequently used honey as a natural antibiotic and skin protectant.Honey contains hydrogen peroxide, which may account for some of its antibacterial properties.It also has a high sugar content, which can help stop the growth of certain bacteria. Additionally, honey has a low pH level. This works to pull moisture away from bacteria, causing the bacteria to get dehydrated and die off.To use honey as an antibiotic, apply it directly to the wound or infected area. The honey can help kill off the bacteria and aid in the healing process.If possible, opt for raw Manuka honey.This form of honey offers the most health benefits. You can purchase raw Manuka honey here. You can also ingest honey to aid in the treatment of internal infections. Simply swallow a whole tablespoon or stir it into a warm cup of herbal tea for a soothing treat. Honey is generally safe to use on the skin or in the body, though you should never give honey to an infant under 1 years old.Instead, consult your healthcare provider for an appropriate alternative.

Garlic Extract

Garlic has long been thought to have antimicrobial properties. A 2011 study found that garlic concentrate is effective against bacteria. You can purchase garlic concentrate or extract at your local health food store. You may also be able to make your own by soaking a few garlic cloves in olive oil. Garlic is generally safe to ingest, but large doses might cause internal bleeding.Up to two cloves per day is considered an acceptable dosage.If you're taking a garlic supplement, be sure to follow the dosage directions as provided. If you're taking blood-thinning medication, consult your healthcare provider before using garlic as an antibiotic. Large doses of garlic can amplify the effects of this medication. You can also apply garlic concentrate directly to a wound or blemish.

Myrrh Extract

Many people are familiar with myrrh, but its ability to ward off harmful germs isn't as widely known.Researchers in a 2000 study concluded that an extract of myrrh could kill off several everyday pathogens. This includes:

- E. Coli

- Staphylococcus aureus

- Pseudomonas aeruginosa

- Candida albicans

Myrrh is generally well-tolerated, but ingesting it may cause diarrhea. If applying myrrh to the skin, it's possible to experience a small skin rash.If consumed in large doses, myrrh may cause heart problems. Myrrh is typically prepackaged, so be sure to follow the dosage instructions on the label.

Thyme Essential Oil

Many all-natural household cleaners use thyme essential oil.This oil has been shown to be especially helpful against antibiotic-resistant bacteria.In a 2011 study, researchers tested the effectiveness of both lavender and thyme essential oil.Both oils were tested in a pool of over 120 strains of bacteria.The researchers found thyme essential oil to be more effective at killing bacteria than lavender essential oil. Thyme essential oil is for external use only.You shouldn't take thyme oil by mouth. Before applying to the affected area, be sure to dilute the essential oil with equal parts carrier oil.Common carrier oils include coconut and olive oils.Applying undiluted essential oil to the skin may cause inflammation and irritation. People with high blood pressure or hyperthyroid problems shouldn't use thyme essential oil.

Oregano Essential Oil

Carvacrol is an ingredient found in oregano essential oil. It has important therapeutic properties that further activate healing in the body when inhaled. Oregano oil has been found to help heal gastric ulcers and reduce inflammation. To treat fungal infections on your skin, add one drop of oregano essential oil per teaspoon of a carrier oil such as olive or coconut oil .Apply the mixture to the affected area. You can also diffuse oregano oil in the air to help clear sinus infections. You shouldn't ingest oregano essential oil or use undiluted essential oil on the skin. You may also be able to eradicate bacteria in the home with a homemade cleaning agent made of:

- Oregano Essential Oil
- Vinegar
- Water
- Lemon

Antiviral Herbs

Common kitchen herbs, such as basil, sage, and oregano, as well as lesser-known herbs like astragalus and sambucus, have powerful antiviral effects against numerous viruses that cause infections in humans.It's easy to add these powerful herbs to your diet by using them in your favorite recipes or making them into teas.

Oregano

Oregano is a popular herb in the mint family that's known for its impressive medicinal qualities.Its plant compounds, which include carvacrol, offer antiviral properties.In a test-tube study, both oregano oil and isolated carvacrol reduced the activity of murine norovirus (MNV) within 15 minutes of exposure. MNV is highly contagious and the primary cause of stomach flu in humans. It is very similar to human norovirus and used in scientific studies because human norovirus is notoriously difficult to grow in laboratory settings. Oregano oil and carvacrol have also been shown to exhibit antiviral activity against herpes simplex virus type-1 (HSV-1); rotavirus, a common cause of diarrhea in infants and children; and respiratory syncytial virus (RSV), which causes respiratory infections.

Sage

Also, a member of the mint family, sage is an aromatic herb that has long been used in traditional medicine to treat viral infections. The antiviral properties of sage are mostly attributed to compounds called safficinolide and sage one, which are found in the leaves and stem of the plant. Test-tube research indicates that this herb may fight human immunodeficiency virus type 1 (HIV-1), which can lead to AIDS. In one study, sage extract significantly inhibited HIV activity by preventing the virus from entering target cells. Sage has also been shown to combat HSV-1 and Indiana vesiculovirus, which infects farm animals like horses, cows, and pigs.

Basil

Many types of basil, including the sweet and holy varieties, may fight certain viral infections. For example, one test-tube study found that sweet basil extracts, including compounds like apigenin and ursolic acid, exhibited potent effects against herpes viruses, hepatitis B, and enterovirus. Holy basil, also known as tulsi, has been shown to increase immunity, which may help fight viral infections. In a 4-week study in 24 healthy adults, supplementing with 300 mg of holy basil extract significantly increased levels of helper T cells and natural killer cells, both of which are immune cells that help protect and defend your body from viral infections.

Fennel

Fennel is a licorice-flavored plant that may fight certain viruses. A test-tube study showed that fennel extract exhibited strong antiviral effects against herpes viruses and parainfluenza type-3 (PI-3), which causes respiratory infections in cattle. What's more, trans-anethole, the main component of fennel essential oil, has demonstrated powerful antiviral effects against herpes viruses. According to animal research, fennel may also boost your immune system and decrease inflammation, which may likewise help combat viral infections.

Garlic

Garlic is a popular natural remedy for a wide array of conditions, including viral infections. In a study in 23 adults with warts caused by human papillomavirus (HPV), applying garlic extract to affected areas twice daily eliminated the warts in all of them after 1–2 weeks.Additionally, older test-tube studies note that garlic may have antiviral activity against influenza A and B, HIV, HSV-1, viral pneumonia, and rhinovirus, which causes the common cold.However, current research is lacking.

Animal and test-tube studies indicate that garlic enhances immune system response by stimulating protective immune cells, which may safeguard against viral infections.

Lemon Balm

Lemon balm is a lemony plant that's commonly used in teas and seasonings. It's also celebrated for its medicinal qualities. Lemon balm extract is a concentrated source of potent essential oils and plant compounds that have antiviral activity. Test-tube research has shown that it has antiviral effects against avian influenza (bird flu), herpes viruses, HIV-1, and enterovirus 71, which can cause severe infections in infants and children.

Peppermint

Peppermint is known to have powerful antiviral qualities and commonly added to teas, extracts, and tinctures meant to naturally treat viral infections. Its leaves and essential oils contain active components, including menthol and rosmarinic acid, which have antiviral and anti-inflammatory activity. In a test-tube study, peppermint-leaf extract exhibited potent antiviral activity against respiratory syncytial virus (RSV) and significantly decreased levels of inflammatory compounds.

Rosemary

Rosemary is frequently used in cooking but likewise has therapeutic applications due to its numerous plant compounds, including oleanolic acid. Oleanolic acid has displayed antiviral activity against herpes viruses, HIV, influenza, and hepatitis in animal and test-tube studies. Plus, rosemary extract has demonstrated antiviral effects against herpes viruses and hepatitis A, which affects the liver.

Echinacea

Echinacea is one of the most popularly used ingredients in herbal medicine due to its impressive health-promoting properties.Many parts of the plant, including its flowers, leaves, and roots, are used for natural remedies.In fact, Echinacea purpurea, a variety that produces cone-shaped flowers, was used by Native Americans to treat a wide array of conditions, including viral infections. Several test-tube studies suggest that certain varieties of echinacea, including E. pallida, E. angustifolia, and E. purpurea, are particularly effective at fighting viral infections like herpes and influenza. Notably, E. purpurea is thought to have immune-boosting effects as well, making it particularly useful for treating viral infections.

Sambucus

Sambucus is a family of plants also called elder. Elderberries are made into a variety of products, such as elixirs and pills, that are used to naturally treat viral infections like the flu and common cold. A study in mice determined that concentrated elderberry juice suppressed influenza virus replication and stimulated immune system response. What's more, in a review of 4 studies in 180 people, elderberry supplements were found to substantially reduce upper respiratory symptoms caused by viral infections.

Licorice

Licorice has been used in traditional Chinese medicine and other natural practices for centuries. Glycyrrhizin, liquiritigenin, and glabridin are just some of the active substances in licorice that have powerful antiviral properties.Test-tube studies demonstrate that licorice root extract is effective against HIV, RSV, herpes viruses, and severe acute respiratory syndrome-related coronavirus (SARS-CoV), which causes a serious type of pneumonia.

Astragalus

Astragalus is a flowering herb popular in traditional Chinese medicine. It boasts Astragalus polysaccharide (APS), which has significant immune-enhancing and antiviral qualities.Test-tube and animal studies show that astragalus combats herpes viruses, hepatitis C, and avian influenza H9 virus. Plus, test-tube studies suggest that APS may protect human astrocyte cells, the most abundant type of cell in the central nervous system, from infection with herpes.

Ginger

Ginger products, such as elixirs, teas, and lozenges, are popular natural remedies — and for good reason. Ginger has been shown to have impressive antiviral activity thanks to its high concentration of potent plant compounds. Test-tube research demonstrates that ginger extract has antiviral effects against avian influenza, RSV, and feline calicivirus (FCV), which is comparable to human norovirus. Additionally, specific compounds in ginger, such as gingerols and zingerone, have been found to inhibit viral replication and prevent viruses from entering host cells.

Ginseng

Ginseng, which can be found in Korean and American varieties, is the root of plants in the Panax family. Long used in traditional Chinese medicine, it has been shown to be particularly effective at fighting viruses. In animal and test-tube studies, Korean red ginseng extract has exhibited significant effects against RSV, herpes viruses, and hepatitis A. Plus, compounds in ginseng called ginsenosides have antiviral effects against hepatitis B, norovirus, and coxsackieviruses, which are associated with several serious diseases including an infection of the brain called meningoencephalitis.

Dandelion

Dandelions are widely regarded as weeds but have been studied for multiple medicinal properties, including potential antiviral effects. Test-tube research indicates that dandelion may combat hepatitis B, HIV, and influenza. Moreover, one test-tube study noted that dandelion extract inhibited the replication of dengue, a mosquito-borne virus that causes dengue fever.This disease, which can be fatal, triggers symptoms like high fever, vomiting, and muscle pain.

Garlic And Honey

Garlic and honey have many proven health benefits.You can enjoy their beneficial properties by using them alone or together. They can be taken as medicinal supplements, or added to recipes in their natural form. Some forms of honey and garlic may be more beneficial than others.

Properties Of Garlic And Honey

Garlic and honey have been used in traditional medicines around the world.The main health ingredient in garlic is allicin. It contains oxygen, sulfur, and other chemicals that give garlic antibacterial and disease-fighting properties. A medical review notes that chopping or crushing fresh garlic cloves releases more allicin than using the cloves whole. However, chopped or crushed garlic can lose its allicin levels quickly. For maximum benefit, you'll want to use fresh garlic as soon as possible. Honey is naturally high in antioxidants called flavonoids and polyphenols.These chemicals help to fight inflammation (redness and swelling) in the body. This can help balance the immune system and prevent certain illnesses. Honey also has antibacterial, antiviral, and antifungal properties.

Health Benefits Of Garlic And Honey

Medical research has investigated the health benefits of garlic and honey alone and in combination. Some of the research is based on claims made in home remedies that have been used for hundreds of years. In traditional Ethiopian medicine, a type of local honey is used to treat breathing problems, skin infections, and even diarrhea. Garlic is traditionally used to treat colds and coughs. It's also reported to boost the immune system and help ease asthma symptoms.Arab traditional medicine recommended garlic to help treat heart disease, high blood pressure, arthritis, toothache, constipation, and infections.

Antibacterial: A lab study found that garlic and a kind of honey called tazma honey were able to stop some kinds of bacteria from growing. The study tested each food separately and as a mixture. Researchers found that garlic and honey were both able to kill the bacteria when tested alone. A combination of garlic and honey worked even better. The garlic and honey combination slowed or stopped the growth of bacteria that cause illness and infections including pneumonia and a kind of food poisoning. These included Streptococcus pneumonia, Staphylococcus aureus and Salmonella. Another lab study showed that a combination of garlic juice and honey was even able to stop types of bacterial infections that cannot be treated by antibiotic drugs. More research is needed to find out if honey and garlic have the same effect against bacterial infections in the human body.

Antiviral: Some kinds of honey also have powerful antiviral properties. This may help treat or prevent colds, flus, and other illnesses caused by viruses. A lab study found that Manuka honey was able to stop the flu virus from growing. The researchers concluded that honey, especially Manuka honey, worked almost as well as antiviral drugs against this virus.

Heart health: Several clinical and lab studies have looked at the many heart health benefits of garlic. The Mayo Clinic notes that antioxidants in honey may also help protect you against heart disease. According to a medical review, garlic acts to help lower the risk of heart disease and stroke by:

- Lowering high blood pressure
- Lowering high cholesterol
- Preventing too much clotting (blood-thinning)
- Preventing hardened or stiff blood vessels

Another review found that the sulfur molecules in garlic may also help protect heart muscles from damage and make blood vessels more elastic. This helps to prevent heart disease, blood clots, and stroke. A type of cholesterol called LDL is the main cause of hardening in the blood vessels. This can lead to heart disease and stroke. Research in rats showed that garlic helped lower harmful LDL cholesterol levels. The rats were fed garlic powder or raw garlic extract. More research is needed to determine if people would have the same cholesterol-lowering benefits.

Memory and brain health: Both garlic and honey are high in antioxidant compounds. These healthy chemicals help to balance your immune system and prevent illness.They may also protect your brain from common diseases like dementia and Alzheimer's. More research is needed on how garlic can prevent or slow these age-related diseases. Studies note that aged garlic extracts contain a high amount of an antioxidant called kyolic acid.This powerful antioxidant may help protect the brain from damage due to aging and disease. This may help improve memory, concentration, and focus in some people.

How to use garlic and honey

You can enjoy the many health benefits of garlic and honey by either cooking with them or taking them as nutritional supplements. Freshly crushed or chopped garlic has the most health benefits. Garlic powder and aged garlic extract are also high in healthy compounds. Garlic oil has fewer health properties, but can still be used to add flavor to cooking. Garlic supplements usually contain garlic powder. There's no recommended dosage for fresh garlic or garlic supplements.

Some clinical studies show that you can get health benefits from a daily dosage of 150 to 2,400 milligrams of garlic powder. Raw, pure honey can be used as a natural remedy for coughs, colds, and sore throats. The Mayo Clinic recommends using citrus honey, eucalyptus honey, and labiatae honey for coughs. Take a spoonful of honey as needed or add honey to herbal teas to help ease cold and flu symptoms. Honey can also be used on the skin to help soothe allergic rashes, acne flare-ups, and other skin irritations. It can also be used to help heal skin wound, burns, and scratches. Cleanse skin and apply a small amount of medical-grade honey directly to the area.

Recipes Using Garlic And Honey

A combination of honey and garlic can boost the flavor and health benefits of many daily recipes.

Salad Dressing: You can make your own salad dressing by mixing olive oil, balsamic vinegar, and dried herbs.Mix in freshly chopped garlic and pure honey to help balance the tartness and add more nutrition. Combine all ingredients in a clean jar and shake well.

Honey-Fermented Garlic: Honey-fermented garlic is a type of "pickled" garlic. It can be stored for up to a month at room temperature. Place peeled whole garlic cloves in a clean and sterile jar.You can sterilize a glass jar and lid by boiling it in water. Pour honey over the garlic and stir to combine. Make sure the garlic is completely covered with honey. Seal the jar and let it sit on a counter for three days. Open the jar to let out any gases and stir the garlic and honey.If you see tiny bubbles in the honey, it means the garlic has started to ferment.Reseal and let sit for at least a week before using.

Honey Garlic Marinade: Honey garlic marinade can be used to flavor chicken, fish, and vegetables. Combine freshly chopped garlic (or garlic powder), honey, low-sodium soy sauce, and olive oil. You can also add other fresh or dried herbs if you wish.Toss chicken or fish in the honey garlic marinade and let sit in the fridge for at least one hour. You can also marinade and freeze poultry and fish for a quick homemade meal when you're too busy to prep food.

Potential Side Effects Of Garlic And Honey

The nutritional and health compounds in garlic and honey may cause side effects or reactions in some people. Talk to you doctor before you take garlic or honey supplements.

Garlic interactions: Garlic can cause allergic reactions in some people. Taking garlic supplements or eating garlic in larger doses can thin your blood and increase the risk of bleeding. For this reason, garlic can cause a negative interaction with medications that thin your blood. These include:

- Salicylate (Aspirin)
- Warfarin (Coumadin)
- Clopidogrel (Plavix)

Garlic may also interfere with an antiviral drug called saquinavir that's used to treat HIV.

Honey Interactions

Consuming honey may increase blood sugar levels in people with diabetes. Speak to a doctor or dietitian before adding honey to your diet regimen. Honey is not known to interact with other drugs, but it can cause allergic reactions in some people. If you're allergic to bee pollen, ask your doctor if eating honey is safe for you. Honey may also contain other kinds of pollen that can trigger reactions like:

- Wheezing
- Coughing
- Face or throat swelling

- Dizziness

- Nausea

- Vomiting

- Weakness

- Fainting

- Sweating

- Skin reactions

- Irregular heart rhythms

Recipes

Homemade Herbal Antibiotic

The next time you come down with strep throat, a UTI or any other bacterial infection, reach for this homemade herbal antibiotic instead of a prescription.

Tools

- Glass jar with lid

- Dropper

Ingredients

- 1/2 cup fresh thyme, chopped

- 1/2 cup fresh rosemary, chopped

- 1/2 cup fresh ginger, chopped
- 1/2 cup garlic cloves, chopped
- Apple cider vinegar

Instructions

- Let the garlic sit, once chopped, for about 10 minutes to release more allicin, the compound responsible for its healing and antibacterial properties.
- After 10 minutes, add all of the herbs to a glass jar and fill with apple cider vinegar.
- Cap with a lid, gently shake the contents, then place the jar in a cool, dark place, like a cabinet.
- Shake once every day for 6 weeks, then use a strainer to strain the tincture into a glass dropper bottle.
- When you feel the onset of a cold, take one dropper full three times a day in a glass of water until it passes.

Super Antibiotic Master Tonic

Ingredients

- as needed raw apple cider vinegar
- 1/4 cup diced onions
- 1/4 cup minced garlic
- 2 tablespoons grated Horseradish

- 2 tablespoons ground turmeric

- 1 large Scotch Bonnet pepper

- 1/4 cup grated ginger

Steps

- Mix all the ingredients in a jar.

- Finely dice the onion

- Grate the ginger

- I used minced garlic

- Add turmeric and grated Horseradish

- Rinse the Scotch Bonnet pepper leave the stem on it. I didn't have a glove so I used the stem to hold it while I finely sliced it.

- Be careful it's very hot

- Then add apple cider vinegar

- Let sit in a cool dark place. After a month strain the liquids. Put liquids into a jar and seal this will last as long as the vinegar will.

- Use the solids in cooking, dry and save for seasonings, or freeze them for later.

Pear Brown Rice

Serves 6

Ingredients

- 3 tablespoons lemon juice
- 2 teaspoons finely chopped garlic
- ¼ teaspoon ground ginger
- ¼ teaspoon ground black pepper
- 2 pears, diced
- 3½ cups cooked brown rice
- ½ cup chopped green onions
- ½ cup diced celery
- 3 tablespoons vegetable oil

Directions

In a small bowl, combine lemon juice, garlic, ginger, and black pepper. Add pears to the mixture and set aside. In a large bowl, combine brown rice and remaining ingredients.Gently fold in pears.Serve immediately or chill in the refrigerator.

Winter Squash And Kale Risotto With Pine Nuts

Serves 4

Ingredients

- 2 teaspoons olive oil
- 1 cup diced yellow onion

- 3 cloves garlic, minced

- 1 cup Arborio or short-grain rice

- 2 tablespoons pine nuts

- 2 (10 oz.) cans of low-sodium, fat free vegetable broth

- 1 (12 oz.) package frozen winter squash, thawed slightly and diced

- 2 cups finely chopped fresh kale

Directions

Heat oil in a large, shallow saucepan over medium heat.Add salt, onion and garlic, and sauté 2 minutes. Stir in rice and pine nuts and toast for about 2 minutes, stirring occasionally. Add ½ cup broth; cook on medium-low heat, stirring often, until liquid is nearly absorbed. Add remaining broth in the first can, ½ cup at a time, stirring often until each addition is nearly absorbed before adding the next. Add diced squash, and from the second can, ½ cup of broth.Stirring often.Add remaining broth, ½ cup at a time as before.Along with the last ½ cup of broth, add the kale. Cook mixture until all broth is absorbed and kale is soft and bright green.

Honey-Glazed Red Pepper With Goat Cheese

Serves 2

Ingredients

- 1 large sweet red pepper, cored and seeded

- ¼ cup thinly sliced onion

- 2 cloves garlic, crushed

- 1 tablespoon olive oil

- 3 tablespoons honey

- 3 tablespoons red wine vinegar

- 2 teaspoons dried basil, crushed

- ½ teaspoon salt

- 2 whole lettuce leaves

- 2 oz. goat cheese

- Toasted baguettes

- Pepper to taste

Directions

Thinly slice red pepper.Sauté pepper, onion and garlic in oil 10 minutes or until onion and pepper are tender.Add honey, vinegar, basil, salt and pepper; cook and stir over medium-high heat until glazed. Serve on lettuce lined plates with goat cheese and toasted baguettes.

Creamy Honey Sesame Dip For Vegetables

Makes 1 cup

Ingredients

- ¾ cup nonfat mayonnaise

- ¼ cup rice vinegar

- ¼ cup honey

- 3 tablespoons toasted sesame seeds

- 1 tablespoon grated fresh ginger root

- 1 small garlic, minced

- ¾ teaspoon oriental sesame oil

- ⅛ teaspoon crushed red pepper flakes

- Salt to taste

Directions

Whisk together mayonnaise, vinegar and honey in small bowl. Add remaining ingredients; mix thoroughly. Dip may be stored tightly covered in refrigerator up to 1 week.

Rose Emma's Eggplant Relish
Ingredients

- 3 cups eggplant, peeled and cut into ½-inch cubes

- ⅓ cup chopped green peppers

- 1 medium onion, minced

- 3 cloves garlic, pressed

- ⅓ cup oil

- 1 (6 oz.) can tomato paste

- 1 (4 oz.) can mushroom stems and pieces
- ½ cup pimiento-stuffed olives
- ¼ cup water
- 2 tablespoons red wine vinegar
- 1½ teaspoons sugar
- 1 teaspoon seasoned salt
- ½ teaspoon oregano
- ¼ teaspoon pepper

Directions

Put eggplant, green pepper, onion, garlic, and oil in a skillet.Cover and cook gently for 10 minutes, stirring occasionally. Add tomato paste, mushrooms with liquid, and remaining ingredients.Cover and simmer 30 minutes.Turn into a covered dish and refrigerate overnight to allow flavors to blend. Serve with crackers and chips.

Spinach Boreks

Ingredients

- 10 ounces frozen spinach, thawed and chopped
- ¼ cup finely chopped scallions
- ¼ cup minced fresh parsley
- 1 tablespoon minced fresh dill

- 2 garlic cloves, minced
- ¾ cup feta cheese, crumbled
- ¼ cup shredded Monterey Jack cheese
- 2 large eggs
- ½ teaspoon nutmeg
- 1-pound phyllo dough, thawed
- ¾ cup unsalted butter, melted
- Salt and pepper to taste

Directions

Squeeze the spinach to remove as much water as possible. In a food processor, combine the spinach, scallions, parsley, dill, garlic, cheeses, eggs, and nutmeg. Season with salt and pepper, and refrigerate for 20 minutes. Once you open the phyllo dough package, work as quickly as possible. Always keep the phyllo sheets covered with plastic wrap and a damp towel to avoid dryness. Cut the phyllo sheets to a 9-by-13-inch square. Brush the edges of one sheet with melted butter and then brush the center. Repeat until you end up with a total of 10 sheets prepared. Place the sheets on the bottom of a greased 9-by-13-inch cake pan. Spread the filling evenly.Repeat this process with 10 more phyllo sheets as explained earlier. Place these sheets on top of the filling and press to set. Cover with plastic wrap and a damp cloth, and refrigerate for 20 minutes. Meanwhile preheat the oven to 350°F. Using a very sharp knife cut 1½-inch squares into the dough. You should end up with 48 pieces. Bake for 45 minutes or until golden brown. Serve immediately.

Green Beans With Tomatoes

Serves 4

Ingredients

- 1-pound green beans, ends trimmed
- 1½ tablespoon olive oil
- ½ cup pearl onions, peeled and halved
- 2 garlic cloves, minced
- 1 cup cherry tomatoes
- 2 pinches minced fresh thyme
- 2 tablespoons minced fresh basil
- 1 tablespoon minced fresh parsley
- Salt and pepper to taste

Directions

Bring to a boil enough water to cover the green beans. Add 1 teaspoon of salt. Add the green beans and bring to a boil. Reduce heat and simmer until cooked through.Drain and set aside.Heat 1 tablespoon of the oil in a sauté pan over medium heat.Add the pearl onions and sauté until golden brown. Add the garlic and cook for 1 minute. Add the green beans, tomatoes, and herbs, and cook until the vegetables are warmed through.Blend in the remaining oil, season with salt and pepper, and serve immediately.

Green Beans With Mushrooms

Serves 4

Ingredients

- 1-pound green beans, ends trimmed
- 1½ tablespoon olive oil
- 1 small onion, sliced (about 4 ounces)
- ½ cup mushrooms, sliced
- 2 garlic cloves, minced
- 2 pinches minced fresh thyme
- 2 tablespoons minced fresh basil
- 1 tablespoon minced fresh parsley
- Salt and pepper to taste

Directions

Place the greens beans in a large pan and fill with enough water to cover them. Add 1 teaspoon of salt and bring to a boil over high heat. Reduce heat and simmer until cooked through.Drain and set aside. Heat 1 tablespoon of oil in a nonstick pan over medium heat. Add the onion and sauté until translucent. Add the garlic, mushrooms, and herbs, and sauté for 2 minutes. Blend in the green beans, and remaining oil.Season with salt and pepper, and serve immediately.

Okra And Green Beans
Serves 6

Ingredients

- 1-pound okra, uncut
- 1 tablespoon olive oil
- 1 medium onion, diced
- 1-pound fresh green beans
- 2 large garlic cloves, crushed then chopped
- 1 cup water
- ½ teaspoon salt
- ½ teaspoon ground pepper
- 1 (6 oz.) Can tomato paste

Directions

Wash okra pods, trim stems, do not remove caps. Rinse well and drain.Wash beans and cut into 3-inch lengths. Combine water, tomato paste, olive oil, onion, garlic, salt and pepper in a sauce pan and mix well. Heat, stirring frequently, until mixture comes to boil. Add okra and beans and additional water if necessary, to almost cover vegetables. Cook until okra and green beans are tender.

Sugar Snap Peas With Garlic
Serves 4

Ingredients

- 1 tablespoon olive oil
- 2 cups sugar snap peas (about 8 ounces)
- 4 garlic cloves, sliced
- 1 lemon
- Salt and pepper to taste

Directions

Remove strings along both lengths of the sugar snap peas.Heat a wok with the olive oil over medium heat. Add the garlic and sauté quickly. Add the sugar snap peas and sauté until tender and crisp. Sprinkle with a little lemon juice, season to taste and serve immediately.

Potato Parsnip Puree
Serves 8

Ingredients

- 8 medium potatoes (about 3 pounds)
- 1 large parsnip (about 6 ounces)
- 3 large garlic cloves, peeled
- ½ cup milk
- 1 tablespoon olive oil
- 1 tablespoon minced fresh parsley
- 1 tablespoon minced fresh chives
- Salt and pepper to taste

Directions

Peel and quarter the potatoes and parsnip.Place them in a deep pan and add enough cold water to cover. Add the garlic cloves, ¼ teaspoon salt, and bring to a boil over high heat. Cook until cooked through, about 20 to 25 minutes.Strain through a sieve, reserving the cooking liquid, and puree with a potato masher. Add the milk and oil, and mix briefly. If too thick, add a little of the reserved cooking liquid to get to the right consistency.Mix in the parsley and chives, season with salt and pepper, and serve immediately.

Rosemary Potato Skewers

Serves 4

Ingredients

- 4 (about 1⅓ pounds), medium red potatoes peeled and cut into
- 1½ inch chunks
- 1 tablespoon olive oil
- 2 teaspoons butter, melted
- 1 tablespoon chopped fresh rosemary or 1 teaspoon dried rosemary
- 1 large clove garlic, minced
- ½ teaspoon salt
- ¼ teaspoon ground black pepper
- 4 (12") skewers (metal or bamboo) soaked in warm water for 30 minutes

Directions

Prepare a charcoal grill or preheat broiler. In a heavy saucepan with tight-fitting lid, cook the potatoes in 2 inches of boiling water until tender, approximately 15 minutes. Drain potatoes; cool slightly and thread onto skewers.In a small bowl, mix together remaining ingredients. Place potato skewers on the grill 3 to 4 inches above the glowing embers.Brush the skewers with the rosemary mixture. Grill, basting and turning several times, until the potatoes are lightly browned, approximately 10 to 12 minutes.

Broccoli With Pumpkin Hummus
Serves 4

Ingredients

- 1 tablespoon almond butter
- 1 teaspoon flaxseed oil
- ½ tablespoon lemon juice
- ½ teaspoon ground cumin
- ¼ teaspoon ground coriander
- 1 cup cooked garbanzo beans
- 1 cup cooked pumpkin puree
- 1 small garlic clove, pureed
- ½ teaspoon paprika
- 1½ pounds broccoli florets
- Salt to taste

Directions

In a food processor, puree all the ingredients, except the broccoli florets until very smooth. Thin out with water as needed.Serve with the broccoli florets.

Roasted Celery With Apples

Serves 4

Ingredients

- 1 large clove garlic, crushed
- 2 tablespoons olive oil
- 1 stalk celery, about 1½ lbs.
- 2 Golden Delicious apples, cored and quartered
- 1 cup apple juice
- ¼ teaspoon ground cinnamon
- ¼ teaspoon salt
- ⅛ teaspoon ground black pepper
- 4 slices toasted Italian bread

Directions

Preheat oven to 375°F.Place garlic and oil in a 13 × 9 × 2-inch baking pan; bake until oil is hot, about 5 minutes. Meanwhile trim base of celery; cut celery stalk crosswise, about 7 inches from base (save top for soups, stews, etc.); cut stalk lengthwise into 4 wedges. Place celery, apples, apple juice, cinnamon, salt and pepper in baking pan; bake, uncovered, until celery is crisp-tender, about 40 minutes, basting with pan juices every 10 to 15 minutes; discard garlic. Serve immediately over Italian bread.

Roasted Radishes And Root Vegetables
Serves 4

Ingredients

- 3 medium sweet potatoes, peeled and cut into 2-inch chunks (about 3 cups)
- 4 medium parsnips, peeled and cut into 2-inch chunks (about 2 cups)
- 2 medium red onions, peeled and quartered
- 12 ounces radishes
- 1 whole head of garlic, cut in half lengthwise
- 2½ tablespoons olive oil
- ½ teaspoon black pepper
- 1 tablespoon fresh or 1 teaspoon dried thyme
- ¼ teaspoon salt

Directions

Preheat oven to 450°F.In a large bowl put potatoes, parsnips, onions, radishes and garlic.Toss with olive oil, salt and pepper. Arrange vegetables in a single layer in a 15 ½" × 10 ½" roasting pan. Bake until vegetables are tender and golden, stirring occasionally, about 45 minutes.Arrange vegetables on a serving platter. Sprinkle with thyme and garnish with thyme sprigs if desired.

Vegetable Curry

Serves 8

Ingredients

- 2 pounds mixed vegetables (French beans, carrots, peas, potatoes and cauliflower)
- 2 onions, chopped
- 10 mild red chilies
- 10 teaspoons poppy seeds
- 7 cloves garlic
- ½ teaspoon turmeric
- 1-inch piece fresh ginger root, grated
- 3 teaspoons melted butter
- ½ teaspoon curry powder
- 7 ounces plain yogurt
- 3 tablespoons whipped cream
- 1 teaspoon sugar
- Salt to taste

Directions

Prepare and cook the mixed vegetables according to their type, breaking or cutting large ones into bite sized pieces. Grind the onions, chilies, poppy seeds, garlic, turmeric and ginger to a paste.Melt butter in a heavy based saucepan.Add the paste and cook for 3 to 4 minutes.Stir in the curry powder and cook for a further few minutes.Then add the vegetables and water. Bring to a boil and cook for a few minutes. Stir in the yogurt, cream, sugar and salt, heat gently then serve hot with pita bread.

Mediterranean Portobello Burger
Serves 4

Ingredients

- 4 teaspoons olive oil
- 4 large Portobello mushroom caps
- 2 garlic cloves, minced
- 4 onion slices
- 8 tomato slices
- 4 teaspoons feta cheese
- 4 tablespoons roasted red bell peppers spread
- 4 teaspoons black olives
- 8 large basil leaves

- Bunch of lettuce leaves, wide enough to wrap the Portobello mushrooms
- Cider vinegar
- Salt and pepper to taste

Directions

Preheat the grill on medium heat. Brush the Portobello mushrooms with olive oil and sprinkle them with pepper. Grill the mushroom caps for 2 minutes on each side. Grill the onion slices. Turn the mushrooms so that the top of the mushroom cap is on the grill. Now you can fill the inside cavity with the red bell pepper spread, garlic, olives, and season to taste. Grill for another minute or two. Place each Portobello mushroom on a bunch of lettuce leaves (cap upside down), add 1 tablespoon feta cheese, 1 grilled onion slice, 2 tomato slices, 2 basil leaves, and sprinkle with vinegar. Close the lettuce leaves to seal and serve immediately.

Papaya Black Beans And Rice

Serves 6

Ingredients

- 2 teaspoons olive oil
- 1 cup chopped red onion

- ½ cup orange juice

- ¼ cup lemon juice

- 2 tablespoons fresh chopped cilantro

- ½ teaspoon cayenne pepper

- 1 cup finely chopped red bell pepper

- 1 cup finely chopped green bell pepper

- 1 medium papaya, peeled, seeded, and diced

- 2 garlic cloves, minced

- 2 (15 oz.) Cans black beans, rinsed and drained

- 6 cups hot cooked brown rice

Directions

Heat oil in large skillet over medium heat. Add all ingredients except beans and rice. Cook for 5 minutes, stirring occasionally until bell peppers are crisp-tender. Stir in beans. Cook about 5 minutes or until heated through.Serve over rice.

Mexican Casserole

Serves 6

Ingredients

- 4 ounces uncooked ziti pasta nonstick cooking spray

- 2 medium onions, chopped

- 1 garlic clove, minced

- 2 medium carrots, finely chopped
- 1 green pepper, chopped
- 1 medium zucchini, chopped
- 1 (16 oz.) can no added salt tomatoes, undrained
- 1 (8 oz.) can no added salt tomato sauce
- 1 teaspoon oregano
- 1 (16 oz.) can black beans, rinsed and drained
- 1 (10 oz.) package frozen corn, thawed
- 2 tablespoon green chilies, chopped
- 8 ounces fat free ricotta cheese
- 4 ounces shredded low-fat Monterey Jack cheese

Directions

Cook ziti according to package directions without salt; drain well. Preheat oven to 375°F. Coat a Dutch oven or large pot with cooking spray. Add onions, garlic, carrots, peppers, and zucchini; sauté over medium heat for 10 minutes, stirring often. Stir in tomatoes, tomato sauce, and oregano. Bring to a boil; reduce heat to low, simmering 15 minutes.Stir in beans, corn, chilies.Cook for 5 minutes. Remove from heat; add pasta and cheeses, tossing gently.Spoon into a 9-inch square baking dish coated with cooking spray. Bake for 30 minutes or until heated through.Let stand 5 minutes before serving.

Mexibean Mock Lasagna
Serves 6

Ingredients

- 2 teaspoons olive oil
- 1½ cup chopped onion
- 3 garlic cloves, minced
- 1 green pepper, coarsely chopped
- 1 red pepper, coarsely chopped
- 1 teaspoon ground cumin
- 2 teaspoons chili powder spice blend
- ⅛ teaspoon cayenne powder
- 1 cup frozen or fresh corn kernels
- 1 (15 oz.) Can dark red kidney beans, rinsed and drained
- 1 (15 oz.) Can black beans, rinsed and drained
- 1 cup no added salt tomato sauce
- 1 (4 oz.) Can diced green chilies, drained nonstick cooking spray
- 6 corn tortillas
- 1 cup fat free ricotta cheese
- ¾ cup low-fat cheddar cheese, shredded

Directions

In large skillet, heat oil over medium high heat. Sauté onion, garlic, and peppers for 5 minutes.Stir in spices and sauté 1 additional minute.Remove from heat.Mix in corn, beans, tomato sauce, and diced green chilies. Spray 13" × 9" dish with cooking spray.Place 3 tortillas in the dish arranging to cover the bottom.Spoon in half of the corn mixture, and spread ½ cup ricotta cheese on top.Sprinkle with half of the cheddar cheese. Repeat layers, using up all the ingredients.Cook, uncovered at 350°F for 45 minutes, until casserole is thoroughly heated and cheddar cheese has melted. Let stand 5 minutes before serving.

Olive Paste And Red Bell Pepper Bruschetta

24 Bruschetta

Ingredients

- 2 large red bell peppers (about one pound)
- 1½ cup pitted black olives
- 2 ounces capers, rinsed and pat-dried
- 4 large garlic cloves, minced
- ½ lemon, juiced
- ½ cup olive oil
- 2 ounces anchovy fillets, rinsed and pat-dried
- 1 french baguette
- Salt and pepper to taste

Directions

Preheat the broiler. Place the red bell peppers on a baking sheet and char on all sides. If you have a gas stovetop, you may char the bell peppers over the flames. Once blackened on all sides, place in a paper bag and seal.Let stand for 10 minutes.Peel and seed the bell peppers. Remove ribs and slice into ½-inch wide strips. In a food processor, puree the olives, capers, garlic, oil, lemon juice, and anchovy fillets. The paste should be smooth and spreadable. If it is too thick, add a little more olive oil. Season with salt and pepper and refrigerate for 30 minutes.With a serrated knife, cut the baguette into ¾-inch-thick slices. Place the slices on a baking sheet. Broil on both sides until golden brown.Cool before use.Spread some olive paste on each bread slice and top with 1 slice of red bell pepper.Serve immediately.

Tomato And Walnut Bruschetta
24 Bruschetta

Ingredients

- 5 large Roma tomatoes (about 1½ pounds)
- 3 ounces fresh mozzarella, finely chopped
- ½ cup walnuts, finely chopped

- 3 large garlic cloves, minced
- ⅓ cup fresh basil, finely chopped
- 1 tablespoon minced fresh oregano
- 2 tablespoons olive oil
- 1 tablespoon balsamic vinegar
- 1 teaspoon lemon juice
- 1 French baguette
- Salt and pepper to taste

Directions

Cut the tomatoes in half. Seed, dice, and place in a bowl. Add the remaining ingredients, except the bread, and toss well. Refrigerate for 2 hours. Preheat the broiler.With a serrated knife, cut the baguette into ½-inch-thick slices. Place the slices on a baking sheet. Broil on both sides until golden brown. Cool before use. Spoon some bruschetta mixture over each bread slice and serves immediately.

Salmon Bruschetta

- 24 bruschetta
- Ingredients
- 1⅓ cup fresh basil
- ⅔ cup fresh parsley

- 2 tablespoons minced fresh lemon thyme

- ½ cup walnuts

- 2 garlic cloves

- 1 lemon, zested and juiced

- ¼ cup olive oil

- 1 country bread loaf

- 24 smoked salmon slices, rolled (about 1 pound 2 ounces)

- Salt and pepper to taste

Directions

In a food processor, puree the basil, parsley, lemon thyme, walnuts, garlic, 1 tablespoon lemon zest, and 1 tablespoon lemon juice.Gradually add the oil until you have a smooth paste. Season with salt and pepper. If too thick, add a little more oil.Preheat the broiler. With a serrated knife, cut the walnut bread into inch-thick slices. Cut each slice in half. Place the slices on a baking sheet. Broil on both sides until golden brown.Cool before using. Spread some paste over each bread slice. Add one salmon roll, sprinkle each with a little lemon juice, and serve immediately.

Stuffed Mushrooms With Tapenade
24 Mushrooms

Ingredients

- 24 large mushrooms, stems removed
- 1 cup pitted black olives
- 1-ounce capers, drained, rinsed, and patted dry
- 2 ounces anchovy fillets
- 4 garlic cloves, minced
- 3 ounces olive oil
- 1 bunch fresh parsley, minced
- 1 teaspoon lemon juice
- Pepper to taste

Directions

Preheat the broiler. Empty and clean the center of each mushroom caps.Place the mushrooms on a baking sheet. Broil for 3 to 4 minutes until the mushrooms start to sweat.Do not overcook, as the mushrooms will start to shrink. Remove from the oven and set aside to cool.In a food processor, puree the olives, capers, anchovies, garlic, oil, and lemon juice. Add pepper to taste. Fill each mushroom cap with the tapenade, sprinkle with parsley, and serve immediately.

Stuffed Bell Peppers
Serves 4

Ingredients

- 1 large tomato (about 5 ounces)
- 4 large red bell peppers
- 1 tablespoon olive oil
- 1 small onion, diced (about 4 ounces)
- 2 garlic cloves, minced
- 10 ounces cooked brown rice
- 3 tablespoons minced fresh parsley
- 2 pinches dried Italian herbs
- 5 ounces vegetable stock (low-sodium)
- 8 ounces tomato sauce
- Salt and pepper to taste

Directions

Make a small X incision at the top and bottom of the tomato. Blanch the tomato for 20 seconds.Place in ice-cold water to stop the cooking process.Peel, seed, and dice the tomato.Bring a large pan of water to a boil. Wash the bell peppers and cut off their tops.Set the tops aside. Remove the seeds and ribs. Parboil the bell peppers by placing them into simmering water for 2 minutes.Then remove the bell peppers from the pan and invert to drain over paper towels. Heat the oil in a nonstick pan over high heat. Add the onion and sauté until translucent. Add the garlic, rice, tomatoes, parsley, Italian herbs, and 3 ounces of the stock, and bring to a boil. Season lightly with salt and pepper and remove from heat. Cool completely.Spoon filling into the bell peppers and finish by replacing their tops.Preheat the oven to 350°F. Place the stuffed bell peppers in a greased pan. Add the remaining stock to the pan and bake for 25 to 30 minutes. Heat the tomato sauce and serve immediately with the stuffed bell peppers.

Wild Rice With Vegetables
Serves 8

Ingredients

- 1⅓ cup wild rice
- 2 teaspoons olive oil
- 2 medium onions, finely diced (about 12 ounces)
- 2 medium carrots, finely diced (about 6 ounces)
- 3 large celery stalks, finely diced (about 6 ounces)
- 1 garlic clove, minced
- 4 cups vegetables stock
- 2 tablespoons minced fresh parsley
- Salt and pepper to taste

Directions

Rinse the rice well and drain.Heat the oil in a deep pan over high heat.Add the onions, carrots, celery, and garlic, and sauté for 2 minutes. Add the rice and sauté for 1 minute. Add the stock and parsley, and bring to a boil. Cover, reduce heat, and cook until tender (approximately 45 minutes but it may depend of the type of rice you use. For best results, see package instructions). Season with salt and pepper and remove from heat. If necessary, strain and serve immediately.